£6.95

The Hoffnung
SYMPHONY ORCHESTRA

Books by
GERARD HOFFNUNG

Hoffnung's The Maestro
The Hoffnung Symphony Orchestra
The Hoffnung Music Festival
The Hoffnung Companion to Music
Hoffnung's Musical Chairs
Hoffnung's Acoustics

The

Hoffnung

Symphony Orchestra

GERARD HOFFNUNG

LONDON 2000

First published 1955
by Dennis Dobson Ltd
2nd impression June 1955
3rd impression November 1955
4th impression February 1957
5th impression October 1957
6th impression June 1958
7th impression June 1960
8th impression November 1962
9th impression December 1968
10th impression December 1972
11th impression October 1975
12th impression December 1977 (Paperback)
13th impression March 1978
14th impression May 1978 (Paperback)
and subsequently re-published
by Souvenir Press from 1983

This edition published 2000
by The Hoffnung Partnership
44 Pilgrims Lane
London NW3 1SN
and reprinted 2004

ISBN 1 903643 01 5

Cover and book design
Vera Brice and Leslie Robinson

Printed and bound in Great Britain
by St Edmundsbury Press Ltd
Blenheim Industrial Park, Newmarket Road
Bury St Edmunds, Suffolk IP33 3TZ

The Hoffnung Symphony Orchestra is the only one of the original set
of these small music books which lacked an inscription.
In this new edition that omission is redressed and the book
is now dedicated whole-heartedly to musicians everywhere:
to orchestras, conductors, soloists, choirs and ensembles,
professionals and amateurs, all of whom delighted the artist
and inspired him to create these timeless drawings.

Acknowledgements

Grateful thanks are due to Sir Peter Ustinov for his contribution
to this book, and also to its designers and printers for the
infinite care and consideration they have taken in its production.

Foreword

Hoffnung means hope, and the artist could not have had a more providential name. His passion for music is well expressed in his wonderful series of caricatures about the orchestra, at times verging on surrealism, at all times imbued with a very personal poetry. Caricature is an art form which unthinking people often put in a category below that of academic portraiture, much in the same way that self-appointed arbiters of literary taste tend to consider the tragic worthier of serious consideration than the comic. Are these valid assessments? I think not.

Any accurate delineation of facial features only succeed in providing a likeness of a kind which a skilful photograph can make more human. The boardrooms of the world are full of such accurate portraits of past managing directors, but it needs the condiment of caricature to make such blandness more lively and, by judicious distortion, more truthful. The portraits of Spanish royalty by Goya, the lawyers of Daumier, and witnesses to the Crucifixion by Matthias Grunewald are redolent of savage observation, and the portraits of Velasquez, Van Gogh and Rembrandt have this same sharpening of focus beyond mere clarity of vision. Hoffnung, and I do not hesitate to mention his name alongside the great artists, does not depend on realism, or on delving beneath its surface. In literary terms, his is the world of the fairy tale, an extension into fantasy of the grim facts of life, or a breath of fresh air in the gloom and pollution of reality. And his genius is to find elements of the same verities in a vision as full of grace notes as the great masters I have mentioned in their researches into the raw side of truth.

Hoffnung and Mozart have things in common. They both died young, and, as a consequence, we found out earlier than we would have normally, that both are immortal. They both dispense felicity and amusement and in the originality of their orchestration, the juxtaposition of sounds or colours, they more than hint at a darker world of fiends and monsters without which the charm and elegance would have no substance.

Peter Ustinov

The Strings

The Violin (Leader)

The Double Violin

The Viola

The Viola Pizzicato

The Yo-Bow

The Cello

7

The Double Bass (a left-handed player)

The Piccolo Double Bass

The Harp

The String Tuba

This instrument is sometimes referred to as the "Minstrel Tuba" or the "Blow Plucker". It is interesting to note that the String Tuba is a member of both the string and brass families though it is usually seated with the former.

The Zither

The Piano (Boudoir Grand)

The Spanish Guitar

The Ondes Martenot

The Woodwind

The Flute and the Piccolo Flute

ƒƒƒ ƒƒƒƒ

The Bass Flute

The Oboe

The Cor Anglais

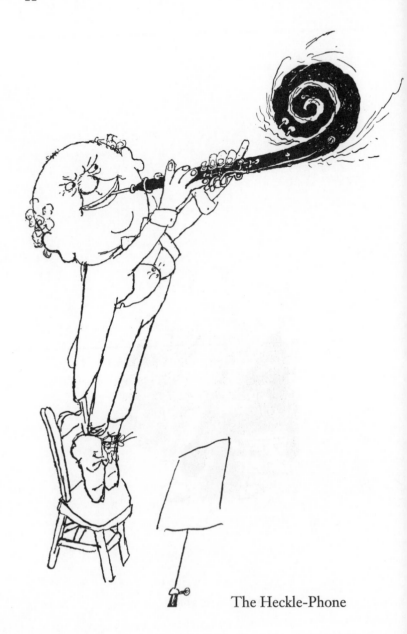

The Heckle-Phone

The Clarinet and the Bass Clarinet

The Saxophone

The Bassethorn

The Bassoon

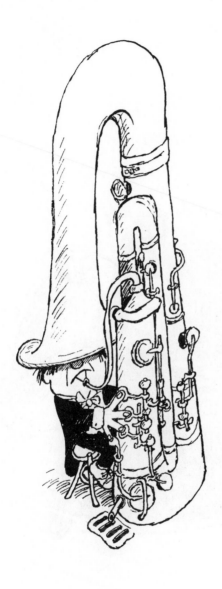

The Contra-Bassoon

The Organ

The Brass

The Horn

30

The Trinkler

The Double Trumpet

The Serpent
For security reasons this
instrument is no
longer in use.

The Trombone

The Bass Trombone

The Wagner Tuba

The Bass Tuba

The Alphorn

The Percussion

The Timpani

The Cymbals

The Side Drum

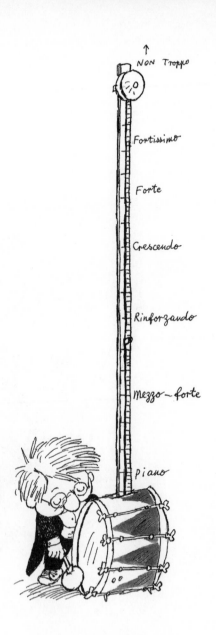

The Bass Drum

The Tum Drum

The Tubular Bells

The Triangle

The Xylophone

The Vibraphone

The Celeste

The Jingle Bells and the Chinese Block

The Wind Machine

The Gong and the Tam Tam

The Castanets